RAND NATIONAL DEFENSE RESEARCH INSTITUTE

T0099296

Building the Guatemalan Interagency Task Force Tecún Umán

Lessons Identified

Gillian S. Oak

Prepared for the Office of the Secretary of Defense

For more information on this publication, visit www.rand.org/t/rr885

Library of Congress Cataloging-in-Publication Data
ISBN: 978-0-8330-8880-2

Published by the RAND Corporation, Santa Monica, Calif.
© Copyright 2015RAND Corporation
RAND® is a registered trademark.

Support RAND
Make a tax-deductible charitable contribution at
www.rand.org/giving/contribute

www.rand.org

Preface

Guatemala is a major transit point for drugs bound for the United States and is the recipient of U.S. counternarcotics aid and technical assistance, much of that provided through U.S. Southern Command (USSOUTHCOM) and U.S. Army South (USARSOUTH). As a first step by Guatemala to improve its counternarcotics capacity, the president of Guatemala established the Interagency Task Force (IATF) Tecún Umán. USOUTHCOM has expressed the intent to apply the IATF as a model to other similarly porous border regions in the area. Thus, documenting and using lessons from the IATF Tecún Umán will help in the development of new and similar units. This report is intended to support that lessons-learned function, demonstrate how these preliminary lessons are being applied to future IATF development, and provide recommendations on how to resolve remaining IATF challenges.

This research was conducted within the International Security and Defense Policy Center of the RAND National Defense Research Institute, a federally funded research and development center sponsored by the Office of the Secretary of Defense, the Joint Staff, the Unified Combatant Commands, the Navy, the Marine Corps, the defense agencies, and the defense Intelligence Community.

For more information on the International Security and Defense Policy Center, see http://www.rand.org/nsrd/ndri/centers/isdp.html or contact the Director (contact information is provided on the webpage).

Contents

Figures

Summary

Guatemala is a major transit point for drugs bound for the United States. Guatemala's Interagency Task Force (IATF) Tecún Umán was established for the interdiction of drug flow across the Mexican border. As part of their counternarcotics missions, U.S. Southern Command (USSOUTHCOM) and U.S. Army South (USARSOUTH) have identified IATF Tecún Umán as one of their top priorities for U.S. support in Central America. USSOUTHCOM believes that this task force, if successful, can serve as a model for others operating along borders in the area, and Guatemala has already begun planning for additional units to provide security on its Honduran (IATF Chortí) and El Salvadoran (IATF Xinca) borders. In support of these efforts, the RAND National Defense Research Institute analyzed progress by IATF Tecún Umán and drew lessons from that experience that can contribute to improved effectiveness of current and future task forces.

The RAND analysis is based on data gathered from papers, briefs, conferences, site visits, and over 20 interviews with U.S. and Guatemalan personnel involved in IATF development and management. An initial set of interviews was conducted and data gathered in December 2013, and a follow-up data-gathering trip was conducted in June 2014 to observe progress over a six-month period. This report identifies key lessons from IATF Tecún Umán and outstanding challenges that still face the IATF. It then provides recommendations to the Guatemalan and U.S. governments on how to overcome those challenges.

History and Status of the IATF

The IATF was not a new concept in Guatemala. There have been several previous attempts at task forces, but they failed to gain traction. This was partly because there was no legal framework in place to create formal commitments from key organizations. This, however, was only one factor. Past efforts were undermined in large part by factors stemming from Guatemala's grim history of military abuse of power, drug trafficking organizations' influence around the country, pervasive corruption, and institutional failure and lack of political will to fix these problems.

Guatemalan President Otto Perez Molina gave his full support for the current IATF concept, that of a task force encompassing the Ministry of Governance (MOG), the Ministry of Defense (MOD), the Superintendencia de Administración Tributaria (SAT, an organization roughly equivalent to U.S. Customs and Border Protection), the Attorney General's Office (Ministerio Público, MP), and the Judicial Agency (Organismo Judicial, OJ). President Molina directed that an Acuerdo—a formal legally binding agreement—be developed to create the framework for the IATF. The Acuerdo was signed on July 25, 2013, and the launch ceremony for IATF Tecún Umán was held on December 16, after the IATF's participation in an operation targeting a major drug trafficking organization. The Acuerdo defines the relationship between the MOG and the MOD and deliberately designates the MOG as the lead organization. However, the Guatemalan government initially set up and staffed IATF Tecún Umán to be predominantly composed of military personnel. This was due to insufficient police capacity, as well as the lack of leadership and experience in senior police ranks to plan and lead operations. The force is expected to become increasingly police-dominated as more police leaders are trained.

IATF Tecún Umán's command element is located in Santa Ana Berlin, with a forward operating base in Tecún Umán on the Mexican border. The base in Santa Ana Berlin was expected to be complete and fully operational in early 2014, but in June, the facilities were still being constructed and the soldiers and police were sleeping in tents. As of June, IATF Tecún Umán was staffed with a total of 231 personnel, consisting of 144 military, 77 police, five customs and border protection agents, and five Judicial Agency representatives. The roles of the various represented agencies in counternarcotics operations were specified in a complex protocol. IATF Chortí HQ will be in Zacapa, with forward operating bases in Morales and Esquipulas, and will have the reverse ratio of military and police from that of IATF Tecún Umán, with 140 military and 200 police, five SAT, and three legal advisors.

Some Key Issues

The most senior levels of the MOD and MOG support the subordination of the IATF completely to the MOG. However, some key leaders remain uncooperative, challenging effective military-police integration at the operational and tactical levels. According to some lower-ranking military personnel, a core problem is competing chains of command: While the MOG is in charge of the IATF, the military personnel involved are still directed through the MOD chain of command. In June 2014, the MOG-MOD relationship was still undefined, and the effects had spread throughout the force. Information gathered from both military and police personnel in Santa Ana Berlin in June 2014 showed segregation and prejudice between the military and police at the operational and tactical levels.

Soldiers were pulled from different brigades to man IATF Tecún Umán. A list of requirements was sent to all the brigades with orders to provide personnel. According to some Guatemalan and U.S. personnel interviewed, the brigades sent whoever was available or could be spared, and not necessarily the personnel best qualified for service in the IATF. However, an exercise assessment conducted by U.S. forces after initial IATF training in July 2013 reported that it was clear that the MOD specially selected company-level leaders for the IATF, and that each company commander and platoon leader was qualified and ready to perform his duties. The police sent veterans to IATF Tecún Umán from an elite counternarcotics force; they were more resistant to compromising and taking orders from military commanders, many of whom were not of the best quality. This resistance caused some tensions among the ranks, especially with the younger soldiers in charge of the units. Since December 2013, the Vice Minister in charge of counternarcotics has worked to steadily replace the older and less flexible police with younger police with expertise more applicable to the IATF and who will work better alongside their military counterparts.

As mentioned earlier, the Santa Ana Berlin base is still not complete. In addition, there have been persistent problems with the existing facilities, resulting in electricity and water outages. Mobile equipment has also been problematic, e.g., U.S.-provided Jeep armored vehicles have been too heavy for the uses to which they are put in Guatemala.

What matters most is whether the unit is effective at achieving its stated mission. As advertised by MOG and MOD leadership in December 2013, IATF Tecún Umán was to serve as an interagency unit capable of planning and executing operations in the border areas. Although the IATF has been participating in operations, its role has been limited to conducting patrols, running checkpoints, and securing perimeters for other units that are actually executing the operations.

Lessons and Main Findings

The IATF as it currently exists is still a nascent and evolving concept, but the Guatemalan government has begun to apply the key lessons already learned to the next IATF—Chortí, situated along the Honduran border—and to planning for additional task forces. Furthermore, these lessons are applicable across a broader spectrum of interagency task forces. They may be summarized as follows:

- Establish the legal framework early. Creating a legal framework and documentation with support from all involved government agencies was crucial for gaining complete cooperation in successfully establishing IATF Tecún Umán. However, the required legal documents were not issued until after the unit had been established and personnel had started working. Had the framework been documented first, many of the growing pains in the interagency relationships might have been avoided.

- Clearly define the interagency relationships. Building and developing the relationship between the police and military is a complex process that takes time, as does establishing and executing a strong relationship with other entities having a smaller presence in the IATF, namely the SAT, MP, and OJ.
- Develop an organic intelligence capability. According to agreement, an Information and Registration Center was to be responsible for collecting and analyzing information used in planning IATF operations. This Center, however, has not been developed. Most of the IATF personnel are capable of gathering their own tactical intelligence, but they have no place to feed it and no support or authority to plan or conduct autonomous operations, thus limiting their ability to react to any intelligence threats discovered. This lesson is being applied at Chortí.
- Transition to police authority and leadership. Although IATF Tecún Umán leadership at the operational level consists of military personnel, police are being trained, educated, and primed to eventually take over the leadership roles. In the meantime, the interim solution of having a predominantly military leadership has created some problems that the Guatemalans are trying to address.
- Identify measures of effectiveness. Despite the limited apparent assessment capability in the office of the Vice Minister for counternarcotics, that office and IATF leadership have made demonstrable progress in collecting data and measures focused specifically on the effects of the operations in which the IATF was involved in the first six months of 2014.
- Communicate purpose and success to the public. Although successful operations and government investment are crucial for IATF sustainment, demonstrating the value of the IATF to the Guatemalan people, especially those near Tecún Umán, is equally important. Because there is no formal designated Guatemalan public information campaign effort, IATF leadership has been working with the U.S. Military Information Support Team in Guatemala City to communicate the benefits of the IATF.

- Prioritize equipment sustainment and maintenance. An important lesson emerging from IATF Tecún Umán was the lack of assigned logistical support. IATF Chortí is planned to have a Service Support Company with mechanics devoted solely to the IATF.

Challenges and Recommendations

The Guatemalan government has made some progress in bringing interagency strengths to bear on the counternarcotics mission through the lessons learned and applied to IATFs Tecún Umán and Chortí. However, several challenges remain to achieve operational effectiveness and political sustainability. Recommendations are provided for both the United States and the Guatemalans to overcome these challenges. The United States has provided significant assistance to the IATFs and has a vested interest in ensuring the units' successes. Thus, the recommendations for Guatemalan action serve as possible milestones of progress that can encourage continued U.S. involvement.

- The duality-of-command issue. *Guatemalan leadership* needs to ensure each level understands and supports associated roles and responsibilities, from the most senior leader to the most junior soldier or police agent on the ground. The *United States* should continue its involvement in resolving this issue.
- Operational planning capability. Because of the lack of operational planning capability at the ministerial level, the IATF has been functioning as a reactionary unit, rather than being able to get out front and execute operations. *Guatemala and the United States* should work together to set up an operational planning cell in the Vice Minister's office and establish an intelligence feedback loop to inform planning.
- Organic training capability. *Guatemala and the United States* should collaborate in developing and executing train-the-trainer

courses to develop the capability to allow Guatemalans to train their own forces.

- Corruption problems. There have been ample problems with police corruption in the past, but efforts are being made to address them. The *United States* should continue to work with the *Guatemalans* on applying stringent vetting to police hires, investigating corruption charges, and ensuring that the police academies are closely complying with new regulations to prevent corruption.
- Finishing the job at Tecún Umán. Guatemala's reason for creating IATF Tecún Umán first was to have a model to learn from and adjust so that IATF Chortí could be done right. However, it now seems as if the Guatemalans have retrenched on their plans for IATF Tecún Umán and are focusing their efforts on Chortí. The *Guatemalans* should refocus on resolving the major problems that prevent IATF Tecún Umán from conducting autonomous operations. Having invested millions of dollars in IATF Tecún Umán, the *United States* should make clear that the development and success of IATF Chortí is tied to that of Tecún Umán.

Conclusion

The Guatemalans have made important strides since the conceptualization of IATF Tecún Umán. Although challenges and outstanding issues between the MOG and MOD remain, the formation of the IATF has helped strengthen interagency cooperation in the counternarcotics mission. To sustain this momentum, continued U.S. investment in developing IATF capabilities is worthwhile, including assisting the successful establishment of IATF Chortí.

MOD	Ministry of Defense (Guatemalan)
MoDA	Ministry of Defense Advisor
MOE	measure of effectiveness
MOG	Ministry of Governance (Guatemalan)
MOP	measure of performance
MP	Ministerio Público
MTT	Mobile Training Team
ODA	Operational Detachment Alpha
OJ	Organismo Judicial
OPORD	Operations Order
PAX	persons
PNC	Policia Nacional Civil [National Civil Police]
RTO	radio telephone operator
SAT	Superintendencia de Administración Tributaria
SCO	Security Cooperation Office
SGAIA	Subdirección General de Análisis e Información Antinarcótica
TCP	Theater Campaign Plan
USARSOUTH	U.S. Army South
USSOUTHCOM	U.S. Southern Command
XO	executive officer

CHAPTER ONE

Introduction

Guatemala is a major transit point for drugs going to the United States. Drugs arrive in Guatemala by sea from Colombia and Ecuador, and then travel by land through Mexico and into the United States. In 2012, it was estimated that more than 80 percent of the primary flow of cocaine trafficked to the United States was first transported through Central America.[1] The Guatemalan-Mexican border is 577 miles long, with only eight official crossing points and an estimated 1,200 blind crossings.[2] This porous border, together with pervasive corruption, has enhanced the ability of international and domestic drug trafficking organizations to transport drugs through Guatemala.

U.S. Southern Command's (USSOUTHCOM) Theater Campaign Plan (TCP) and the USSOUTHCOM Commander have identified Guatemala as a government that can effectively put U.S. assistance to work while also demonstrating the political will to develop its own capacity. A key example of that will and capacity is the Interagency Task Force Tecún Umán (Fuerza de Tarea Tecún Umán, hereafter IATF Tecún Umán), which was developed by President Otto Perez Molina as an initial step in preventing drug flow into and out of Guatemala. Operational since July 2013, it is the first interagency unit of its type to receive the kind of support needed from the relevant Guatemalan government agencies to enable participation in operations. Cen-

---

[1] U.S. Department of State, Bureau of International Narcotics and Law Enforcement Affairs, *Guatemala*, 2013 International Narcotics Control Strategy Report, March 5, 2013.

[2] Jennifer Griffin, "America's Third War: Fighting Drug Cartels in Guatemala," Fox News, December 13, 2010.

tered on San Marcos and Quetzaltenango, IATF Tecún Umán is situated and organized to patrol the Guatemalan-Mexican border and was designed to investigate and interdict illicit trafficking operations and arrest those involved. The IATF was designed to unify the efforts of air, maritime, and land interdiction operations. Its interagency approach had not previously been proven successful in Guatemala.[3]

USSOUTHCOM has also expressed the intent to apply the IATF as a model to other similarly porous border regions in the area, if it proves successful and if the political will exists in other countries. Indeed, the Guatemalans have already begun planning for additional IATF units along the Honduran (IATF Chortí) and El Salvadoran (IATF Xinca) borders. In fact, President Molina has directed that IATF Chortí be fully operational by the end of 2014, and the plans are in place to develop, train, and set up this new unit. Thus, documenting and using lessons from the IATF Tecún Umán will help in the development of new and similar units. This report is intended to support that lessons-learned function, demonstrate how these preliminary lessons are being applied (or not) to future IATF development, and provide recommendations on how to resolve remaining IATF challenges. We conclude that although the implementation of IATF Tecún Umán continues to face challenges, the experience offers lessons, both positive and negative, that can be helpful in the development of similar units. Moreover, the Guatemalans have begun applying some of the most substantive lessons from IATF Tecún Umán to IATF Chortí and additional IATFs in an attempt to learn from past mistakes. Thus, the IATF concept in Guatemala seems to be making progress toward institutionalization. However, to determine whether the program is truly successful will require continued monitoring. The Guatemalans must ensure that key lessons from IATF Tecún Umán continue to be applied to the unit and future IATF development, and that key institutional problems are addressed and resolved. The United States has an important role to play in continuing to support these efforts.

---

[3] "Interagency Border Unit," Brief, April 3, 2013 (received from the U.S. Security Cooperation Office [SCO]).

This report is based on information gathered from Guatemalan government documents, open-source material, site visits to IATF Tecún Umán bases, interviews with IATF Tecún Umán personnel and Guatemalan officials managing the unit, interviews with personnel in the U.S. SCO in Guatemala involved in setting up the unit, interviews with U.S. military personnel who conduct training for IATF Tecún Umán, and integration of data gathered from briefs and conferences. It is based on two separate data gathering efforts, one in December 2013, and a follow-up visit in June 2014. The data gathered in June 2014 were intended to represent six months of progress by IATF Tecún Umán, as well as lessons and applications of these lessons to IATF Chortí.

Because of this study's limited scope, and because IATF Tecún Umán is still developing and evolving, this report is intended neither to provide a comprehensive assessment of the unit, nor to define specific measures of effectiveness. Rather, it presents lessons identified from the experience of IATF Tecún Umán, discusses how those lessons have been applied to IATF Chortí and can be applied to additional IATF units, identifies remaining challenges to successful IATF development, and provides recommendations for addressing these challenges and for continued U.S. involvement.

to gain traction. The prevailing opinion from both Guatemalan and U.S. personnel involved was that they failed because there was no legal framework in place to create formal commitments, and thus support buy-in, on the part of key organizations. The absence of a formal legal framework, however, was only a minor reason previous efforts at creating interagency task forces failed. Past efforts have been undermined in large part by factors stemming from Guatemala's grim history of corruption and militarization, combined with the increasing influence of drug trafficking organizations around the country and institutional failure and lack of political will to fix these problems. It would be impossible to understand the problems and growing pains of this most recent task force effort without first discussing those issues.

The Guatemalan military's history of corruption, close connections with criminal activity and drug trafficking organizations, and human rights abuses has left Guatemalans understandably wary of any military participation in domestic security. Memories of atrocities committed by the military are still vivid. Throughout the country's bloody 36-year internal conflict, the military dominated Guatemala's political, economic, and social spaces. One of its main strategies to maintain this dominance was "to terrorize and fragment society" by targeting and committing acts of genocide against the Mayan population in poor and rural areas.[2] Corruption and nepotism reached from junior officers to top military leadership, and the military was complicit in criminal activity throughout the country."[3] Border checkpoints like Tecún Umán and El Carmen became the central focus of military intelligence. On paper, their objective was to prevent the guerrillas from smuggling arms and other materials. In practice, the complicity of military personnel meant that they in fact facilitated the trade of Colombian drugs and weapons. Indeed,

---

[2] International Crisis Group, *Guatemala: Squeezed Between Crime and Impunity*, Latin America Report No. 33, June 22, 2010, p. 3.

[3] Julie López, "Guatemala's Crossroads: Democratization of Violence and Second Chances," Working Paper Series on Organized Crime in Central America, Woodrow Wilson Center for International Scholars, December 2010, p. 11.

during the 1980s, Guatemalan military intelligence developed an "institutional monopoly" over illicit trafficking throughout Guatemala. Colombian traffickers used Guatemalan networks comprising military intelligence officials, their subordinates, informants, and partners to move large amounts of cocaine into Mexico.[4] This trafficking network remained in place after the Firm and Lasting Peace Accord in 1996 and, along with other such networks, continued to operate along the rural border regions with impunity as a weak federal government did little or nothing to stop it.

Government corruption grew even worse after the war was over, and organized criminal groups became even more influential in numerous government departments.[5] Some reforms were instituted. Military personnel numbers dropped from 44,000 in 1997 to 16,000 in 2009. The government made a commitment to reform and rebuild the civilian police force. However, this proved easier said than done: The new National Civil Police (PNC) failed to sufficiently or effectively fill security gaps.[6] The PNC grew from 12,000 in 1996 to about 25,000 in 2013. However, the police do not have the trust, confidence, or cooperation of the Guatemalan citizens, because of known problems with information leaks and an inability to protect witnesses.[7]

Both corruption and involvement in trafficking and criminal activity persist within the military and police.[8] As the influence and dominance of the Colombian DTOs decreased in the late 1990s, Mexican cartels began to fill the void. Tecún Umán remains a known

---

[4] Center for Naval Analysis (CNA), "Criminal Organizations and Illicit Trafficking in Guatemala's Border Communities," IPR 15225, December 2011, pp. 10–11.

[5] López, 2010, p. 17.

[6] CNA, 2011, p. 13.

[7] A United States Agency for International Development study found that the public had less confidence in the police than in any other justice sector institution. The police scored 31 on a 1 to 100 scale of confidence in political institutions, whereas the army scored 56. International Crisis Group, *Guatemala: Drug Trafficking and Violence*, Latin America Report No. 39, October 11, 2011, p. 11.

[8] According to the CNA report, there is an "abundance of evidence" that criminal organizations have penetrated the highest levels of the Guatemala military and police (CNA, 2011, p. 14).

illicit trafficking area. DTOs and drug lords have a profound influence among the people there. Often they, not government forces, maintain a level of security in the area, which helps support continued trafficking of illicit drugs, weapons, and materials. In addition, corruption and collaboration with the DTOs by local civilian authorities in Tecún Umán are reported.[9] This widespread influence by DTOs and cartels has also stymied any previous efforts to create a legitimate interagency task force to provide security and counter illicit trafficking.

In this context, it is perhaps not surprising that both political will and commitment from the Guatemalan government to fill the institutional vacuum, weed out corruption, and develop strong organizations to counter the DTOs have been lacking. A change came with the election of President Molina, who made these his top priorities. On a state visit to the United States in early 2012, the Guatemalan administration requested U.S. assistance to help with the rapidly proliferating influence of the Mexican cartels in Guatemala. The United States began engaging in regular defense institution building efforts to reform the Guatemalan institutions, assisting in the development of a National Defense Strategy, and advising on anticorruption measures. In all these efforts, President Molina offered full support and strictly enforced improvements in his agencies and departments.

President Molina gave his support for the current IATF concept as part of his effort to counter illicit trafficking and fight violent crime in border regions.[10] The interagency aspect, namely the coordination and collaboration between the army, police, SAT, MP, and OJ, provides the crucial difference that could yield more effective border patrol than these agencies operating separately. As things stand, each organization on its own is insufficient: The police are the only entity legally authorized to arrest and detain any individual, but the force is still largely ineffective and lacks the leadership or experience of the mili-

---

[9]   CNA, 2011, p. 5.

[10]   U.S. Department of State, Bureau of International Narcotics and Law Enforcement Affairs, *Country Report: Guatemala*, 2014 International Narcotics Control Strategy Report, 2014.

tary. Although the police are authorized to search vehicles, only SAT is allowed by law to open and search any locked containers. However, they need to first obtain a warrant from MP and OJ in order to do so. Finally, an individual can be detained for only a limited amount of time before he is charged, and the MP and OJ must try to sentence that individual in a timely manner. Thus, having all entities in the same geographic area is a huge benefit to efficient and effective countertrafficking operations.

One of the first ways President Molina set the IATF Tecún Umán apart from previous task force efforts was that he directed the development of an Acuerdo—a formal legally binding agreement—to create the framework for the IATF. This framework went through many revisions and rewrites. The IATF Working Group, which included key representatives from MOD, MOG, SAT, MP, and OJ, met weekly for over 18 months. This working group planned the concept of the IATF structure, reached a consensus about IATF management, and wrote what became the Acuerdo Gubernativo No. 277-2013 that created IATF Tecún Umán (see Appendix).

The Acuerdo for IATF Tecún Umán was signed by the Minister of Governance, the Minister of Defense, and President Molina on July 25, 2013. It defines the role of IATF Tecún Umán as "conducting combined security operations throughout Guatemala to prevent, combat, dismantle, and eradicate criminal actions." It specifically directs the integration of the MOD and MOG in the unit and outlines the authority of IATF Tecún Umán to coordinate with SAT, MP, and other state institutions as necessary. SAT, MP, and OJ were intentionally kept at a coordination level in the Acuerdo, rather than designated official signatories. This was done to elicit their buy-in and participation in IATF Tecún Umán, since SAT, MP, and OJ wanted organizational independence if they were to come to the table and agree to be a part of IATF Tecún Umán operations.

The Acuerdo defines the MOG-MOD relationship and deliberately designates the MOG as the lead agency to emphasize that the IATF is conducting a police mission with the military in the support role. However, the Guatemalan government initially set up and staffed IATF Tecún Umán to be MOD-heavy. This was due to insufficient police capacity, as well as the lack of leadership and experience in senior police ranks to plan and lead operations. As more police leaders are trained, the force is expected to become increasingly police dominated. In the meantime, the concept of MOG leadership is understood by both the MOG and MOD. From an operational perspective, it means that only the 5th Vice Minister (who is in the MOG chain of command) can give the order to deploy IATF Tecún Umán for a mission.

The first complement of IATF Tecún Umán personnel completed their 15-week initial training on June 28, 2013, and began movement to their headquarters in Santa Ana Berlin in July 2013. They originally planned to be fully operational as of August 8, 2013. However, on July 12, the unit was called upon by President Molina to participate in Operación Dignidad, which targeted the Villatoro-Cano Drug Trafficking Organization. During this operation, IATF Tecún Umán carried out numerous arrests and confiscations of property, money, and equipment from Villatoro-Cano, all based on Government of Guatemala intelligence. The IATF Tecún Umán launch ceremony was eventually held on December 16, 2013. There, IATF Tecún Umán displayed its capabilities in the land, sea, and air contexts, demonstrating simulated drug interdiction and demolition of narcotics facilities. President Molina and leadership from MOG, MOD, and SAT, among other organizations, all attended and spoke about the importance of IATF Tecún Umán capabilities.

IATF Tecún Umán is part of a strategic vision of the Governmental Pact of Security, Justice, and Peace. Under this plan, there are three types of task forces. First, the *thematic task forces* focus on specific topics, such as kidnapping and trafficking. Second, *specific territorial task forces* focus on "red" (high threat) areas. These task forces will be mobile and deployable to areas around the entire country. Finally, *border protection task forces*, such as Tecún Umán and Chortí, are intended to be based and conduct operations in their designated border regions. In addition to these and Xinca, along the El Salvadoran border, there are three more border protection task forces planned: one on the Belize border (Balam) and two additional IATFs on the Mexican border. The plan is to have an IATF administrator for each task force, with one senior administrator overseeing all of them.

Location and Organization

IATF Tecún Umán's command element is located in Santa Ana Berlin, with a forward operating base in Tecún Umán. The base in Santa Ana Berlin was expected to be complete and fully operational in early 2014, but in June 2014, the facilities were still being constructed and the soldiers and police continued to sleep in tents. The explanation for this would require a further investigation of the causes of failure to complete the facilities on time; however, it seems to at least be in part because of unclear and therefore uncoordinated resourcing chains between the MOG and MOD. The forward operating base in Montañita was to be set up and operational in 2014; however, because of disagreements between the MOG and MOD chains of command, this has been indefinitely delayed. Figure 2.1 presents a map of the locations of the current and planned IATF Tecún Umán bases.

As of June 2014, IATF Tecún Umán was staffed with a total of 231 personnel, consisting of 144 military, 77 police, five SAT agents, and five OJ representatives. These numbers are constantly in flux, but the organization is consistent: two companies, each with a military commander, comprising SAT agents, three platoons of military; police; and five vehicles. Although there was an intended police advisor position for each company commander, these positions had not, as of June 2014, been filled. Figure 2.2 depicts a basic organizational chart of IATF Tecún Umán as designed (not all billets are filled yet).

IATF Chortí HQ will be in Zacapa, with forward operating bases in Morales and Esquipulas, and a motor pool facility in Finca El Triunfo. Figure 2.3 presents a map of the locations of the planned bases.

The plan for IATF Chortí is to have the reverse ratio of military and police from that of IATF Tecún Umán, with 140 military and 200 police, five SAT, and three legal advisors (see Figure 2.4 for a proposed organizational structure).

Figure 2.1
Map of IATF Tecún Umán Locations

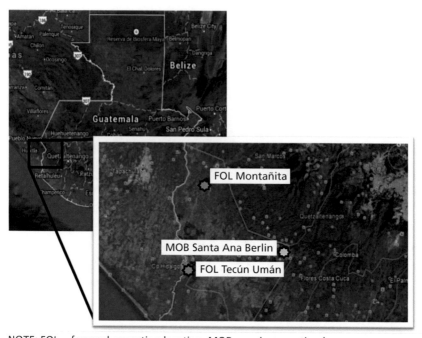

NOTE: FOL = forward operating location; MOB = main operating base.

RAND *RR885-2.1*

Figure 2.2
IATF Tecún Umán Organizational Chart

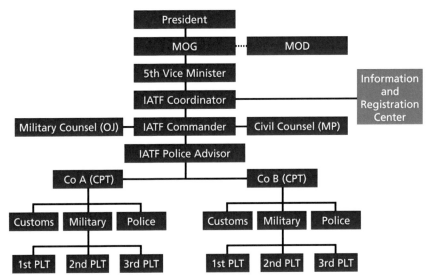

SOURCE: Adapted from Guatemalan Ministry of Governance, "Presentación Fuerza Tarea Tecún Umán," briefing, July 8, 2013.
NOTE: Co A = Company A; Co B = Company B; CPT = captain; PLT = platoon.
RAND RR885-2.2

Figure 2.3
Map of IATF Chortí Locations

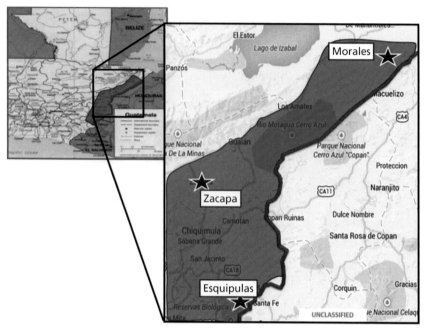

SOURCE: Adapted from U.S. Security Cooperation Office–Guatemala, "IATF-Chortí,"
brief, June 9, 2014.

RAND RR885-2.3

Figure 2.4
IATF Chortí Organizational Chart (Proposed)

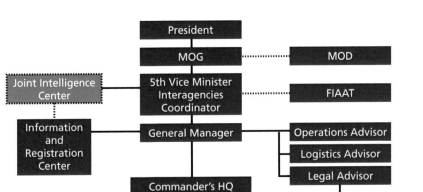

SOURCE: Adapted from U.S. Security Cooperation Office–Guatemala, "IATF-Chortí," brief, June 9, 2014.
NOTE: FIAAT = Interagency Antinarcotics and Antiterrorism Force (Guatemala); A CO = A Company; B CO = B Company; C CO = C Company.

RAND RR885-2.4

CHAPTER THREE

Discussion of IATF Evolution

As of the writing of this report, IATF Tecún Umán has been operational for one year. Although the Guatemalans have begun to apply some key lessons to the establishment of IATF Chortí, challenges remain to be addressed. This chapter discusses observations gathered regarding the IATF evolution between December 2013 and June 2014, and subsequent chapters will present lessons and remaining challenges for IATF development.

MOD-MOG Duality of Command

The most senior levels of the MOD and MOG have bought into and support subordinating the IATF completely to the MOG. However, some key leaders, particularly at the Estado Mayor (National Defense General Staff) level and below, remain uncooperative, challenging effective military-police integration at the operational and tactical levels. According to some lower-ranking military personnel, a core problem is competing chains of command: While the MOG is in charge of the IATF, the military personnel involved are still directed through the MOD chain of command. Indeed, the IATF Coordinator notifies the Chief of National Defense General Staff (CHOD) before conducting operations, even though that is not required by the Acuerdo. The MOD then sends an operations order (OPORD) down the military chain of command. Military personnel below the IATF Coordinator level agree that they need such an order to execute the operation. At the same time, the MOG sends parallel orders down the IATF channels.

MOG staff report that they notify the MOD channel as a courtesy to MOD leadership, even though doing so is not technically legally required for the IATF to conduct operations. Aside from the inherent duplication of effort, this practice also preserves the subordination of military personnel in the IATF to the MOD, rather than to the MOG-led IATF chain of command.

During the initial visit in December 2013, this dual chain of command was identified as a potential source of tension that needed to be resolved. This duality of command, depicted in Figure 3.1, has impeded the ability of IATF Tecún Umán to conduct intended missions and execute operations to its full potential. Essentially, the duality of command problem can be understood in three related ways. First, the MOD and MOG leadership overseeing the IATF have failed to agree on or proliferate roles and relationships through their separate chains of command. Second, at the operational level, it has led to contradictory orders from MOD and MOG chains, jeopardizing operations. Third, at the tactical level, personnel on both sides have not felt compelled to obey orders from the other side.

Figure 3.1
IATF Tecún Umán Duality of Command

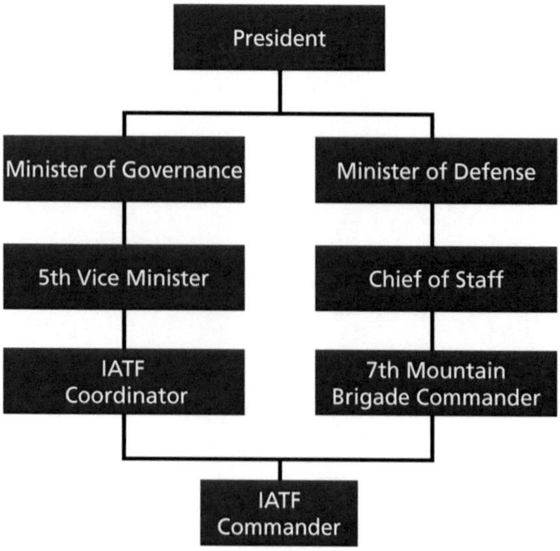

President

Minister of Governance

Minister of Defense

5th Vice Minister

Chief of Staff

IATF Coordinator

7th Mountain Brigade Commander

IATF Commander

RAND *RR885-3.1*

In December 2013, this problem was limited to the senior leadership (there was infighting at the senior MOG and MOD levels), but the effects had not trickled down to the soldiers and police on the ground. Six months later, the MOG-MOD relationship was still undefined, and the effects had spread throughout the force. Information gathered from both military and police personnel in Santa Ana Berlin in June 2014 showed a clear segregation and prejudice between the military and police at the operational and tactical levels. Part of the problem was that leadership on both sides failed to set positive examples for coordination and was negatively influencing personnel by discouraging cooperation. If this issue is left unresolved, it will at best propagate tension, while at worst it could lead to ineffective command and control and jeopardize missions.

The problems begin at the strategic level because MOD and MOG leadership have not agreed on or educated the subordinates in their chains of command about the appropriate roles and relationships between the military and police, and consequences of not complying. The Chief of Staff promised a meeting between the 5th Vice Minister's office and the 7th Mountain Brigade Commander to delineate roles and responsibilities, but as of June 2014, this meeting had not yet occurred. This meeting would go a long way toward solving the chain-of-command problem if it could create a common understanding among all involved parties, but many interviewees agreed that it has been difficult to get and keep the MOD leadership and chain of command engaged regarding the IATF. It seems as though the MOG has been involving leadership in earlier stages of planning for IATF Chortí, but the MOD remains resistant to participation and has not been sending the appropriate level of leadership to planning meetings.

At the operational level, the IATF Tecún Umán Commander is in a difficult position. Guatemalan and U.S. sources alike expressed the view that he is at the unfortunate nexus where the dual-command problem translates from leadership tensions to operational confusion and ineffectiveness, and he bears the brunt of the tensions from above. Although he is in the military chain of command (under the 7th Mountain Brigade Commander), his operational superiors are the IATF Coordinator and 5th Vice Minister. Thus, it is not uncommon for him to receive conflicting orders from the two chains, leaving him in a very difficult position of having to make a decision and, inevitably, get reprimanded by leadership in one of the chains. Several people interviewed expressed their opinions that this position has harmed the commander's career.

At the tactical level, the military and police are segregated in everything they do. The military side shared frustrations over inability to discipline police who had broken rules and dissatisfaction with the level of discipline demanded by the police leadership attached to the IATF. One of the senior military commanders said that early on he had really tried to integrate the military and police, forcing them to mix in the barracks and conduct physical training together, but had been continually challenged and discouraged over the previous six months, so had given up and let them be separate. Military personnel complained that the police did not understand or try to comply with their chain of command, while they admitted that they did not understand how the police chain of command worked. The military explained that they cannot discipline or punish any police who break their rules.

The police asserted that they understood the military chain of command, but that they were a separate entity and had their own sets of rules with which to comply. The police also shared frustrations about the inability to have any authority whatsoever over the soldiers, despite the fact that the Acuerdo states that MOG, and the police in particular, is supposed to be in the leadership role. There was a great deal of pointing fingers from both sides, but ultimately the problems came down to the same source: the absence of a clear definition of the roles and relationships between the military and police at the operational and tactical levels. Until the leaders at the MOD and MOG levels agree on this, this issue will not be resolved.

There are several outstanding issues exacerbating tensions between the military and police at the tactical level that require leadership agreement and direction to resolve. First, leave cycles differ between the military and police. Police work cycles are eight days on, eight days off. Military cycles, by contrast, are 20 days on, ten days off. In December 2013, IATF leadership had expressed intent to bring everyone in line to a single cycle (most likely based on the military cycle), but this had not yet been resolved in June 2014, and the divergent patterns make it difficult to maintain the necessary consistency and equality between the two forces. This has a very tangible operational effect—for example, if a police employee's leave coincides with an operation, new police rotate in and have to be retrained on the entire operation. Second, the service requirements differ between the two entities. Military conscription is for two years, but with a six-month basic training course, the longest they can be assigned anywhere is 18 months. In contrast, the police are assigned to IATF Tecún Umán indefinitely. Finally, there is a substantial disparity in pay that several soldiers mentioned as a source of contention. The police attached to IATF Tecún Umán get incentive pay for being attached to that unit and get a total of 4,000 quetzales (about $500) a month, compared to the soldiers' 1,500 quetzales (about $200) a month.

In December 2013, there was potential for tensions between the military and police attached to IATF Tecún Umán operating at the tactical level because of lack of understanding of their roles and relationships. Thus, from the IATF Commander down the chain, regulations should exist that define specifically each agency's and unit's role within the IATF and the relationships vertically and horizontally. In other words, the regulations should define the chains of command as well as coordination mechanisms within IATF units, including relationships between military and police counterparts. These regulations had been either not completed or not sufficiently disseminated across the IATF, because the lack of understanding of roles and relationships was apparent in December and more substantial in June 2014.

Training

IATF Tecún Umán received a 15-week initial training course, incorporating training by the Guatemalans, Texas National Guard, U.S. Army South (USARSOUTH), and Customs and Border Protection. Since then, the Guatemalans have outlined the following specific Mission Essential Tasks (METs) for the IATF: Command and Control; Area Security; Zone Reconnaissance; Checkpoint Operations; Cordon and

Search; and Quick Reaction Force. Based on these METs, the IATF has received many different types of training from the Joint Planning Assistance Team (JPAT) of the U.S. Security Cooperation Office Guatemala; USARSOUTH; the Texas National Guard (1st Squadron, 124th Cavalry Regiment); the U.S. Customs and Border Patrol; and an Operational Detachment Alpha (ODA) team from U.S. Special Operations Command South (USSOCSOUTH). IATF Tecún Umán has received periodic training from these entities from one to three weeks at a time, covering a wide range of topics:

- weapons familiarization and qualification (small arms and machine gun)
- driver training
- vehicle maintenance
- communications (radio operations)
- mounted and dismounted operations
- vehicle and personnel searches
- traffic checkpoints
- area, zone, and route reconnaissance
- convoy operations
- human rights and rules of engagement
- military operations in urban terrain (MOUT)
- civil disturbance and crowd control
- personnel recovery training
- small unit tactics
- defensive tactics and arrest techniques
- tactical intelligence.

U.S. Army trainers conducted a military tactical intelligence and route reconnaissance course for IATF Tecún Umán in June 2014. Three iterations of classes were taught to two platoons in each class. The training culminated in an exercise where IATF Tecún Umán soldiers and police had to work together to gather intelligence and apprehend and detain a subject. U.S. trainers were impressed with the level of capability and leadership exhibited by the IATF Tecún Umán personnel (both military and police) and commented that although they

noticed segregation between the two, they were professional and operated well together.

In June 2014, the Final Planning Conference was completed for
IATF Chortí's initial training cycle, which was conducted from July
16 to September 14, 2014. This ten-week initial training cycle was conducted by a combination of Guatemalan instructors, USARSOUTH,
48th Infantry Brigade Combat Team (IBCT), and USSOCSOUTH
ODA. In addition, the Guatemalans introduced a "Week 0" into this
initial training—an entire week devoted to integrating the military
and police and forging relationships between those who will serve
together in the IATF.

Leadership and Personnel

Despite MOG authority over IATF Tecún Umán as a whole, both the
leadership of IATF Tecún Umán itself, from the Commander down,
and all command authority are military. The joint S1 (Personnel) and
S4 (Logistics) Department has a military lead, as does the joint S2
(Intelligence) and S3 (Operations) Departments. There is a police Sub-
Inspector, which is roughly equivalent to the rank of sergeant in the
Guatemalan Army, who acts as the leadership for the police personnel
at the Santa Ana Berlin base. In June 2014, it was reported that there
were two police officers assigned as police leadership. However, the
effects of their leadership were neither observed nor documented.

To man IATF Tecún Umán, soldiers were drawn from different brigades. The brigades received orders to provide personnel meeting a list of qualifications. According to some Guatemalan and U.S.
personnel interviewed, the brigades sent whoever was available or
could be spared, and not necessarily the personnel best qualified for
service in IATF Tecún Umán. However, the capstone exercise assessment, conducted by U.S. forces after initial IATF Tecún Umán training in July 2013, reported that it was clear that the MOD specially
selected company-level leaders for the IATF, and that each company
commander and platoon leader was qualified and ready to perform his
duties. Just the same, very little initiative and leadership were observed

below the platoon-leader level. In addition, the assessment noted that the police rarely demonstrated leadership, as the leaders in the units were all MOD.[1] The police in the IATF are all Subdirección General de Análisis e Información Antinarcótica (SGAIA), a Guatemalan elite antinarcotics police force, who receive separate training and vetting (in addition, both military and police go through an IATF-specific vetting process, which was developed by the 5th Vice Ministry and the U.S. SCO). The police sent veterans to IATF Tecún Umán, who were older and more biased, and many were not of the best quality. This caused some tensions among the ranks, especially with the younger soldiers in charge of the units.

Since December 2013, the 5th Vice Minister has worked to steadily replace the older and less flexible police with younger police, with expertise more applicable to IATF Tecún Umán, who will work better alongside their military counterparts. In addition, the 5th Vice Minister's office selected 200 of the best police candidates from the police academy to man IATF Chortí. They were selected in March 2014, went through the antinarcotics police course from March to July, and then integrated with the military for the initial IATF training beginning in July.

Equipment and Facilities

The U.S. has assisted with IATF Tecún Umán equipment, providing 42 Jeep J8 armored vehicles with extensive radio and communications equipment. However, the Jeep vehicles have had numerous problems because their armor is too heavy to be driven the long distances for which they are currently being used. As a result, continual maintenance has been required. This has been burdensome because IATF Tecún Umán had only one mechanic; the unit has had to request three additional mechanics, currently on loan from the MOD. In addition,

---

[1]   "Inter Agency Task Force (IATF) Tecún Umán—Guatemala (GTM) CAPSTONE Exercise Assessment–G3, Current Operations, Counter Transnational Threats (CTT), Counter Transnational Organized Crime (CTOC)," conducted by U.S. Army South G3 CUOPS-Counter Transnational Organized Crime (CTOC), July 2013.

although the MOG has the funding authority for IATF Tecún Umán, all the equipment belongs to the military. The armored vehicles have 7.62mm machine guns, which can be operated only by the military, putting limitations on how much authority the police can have over vehicles during operations.

There are enduring problems with IATF Tecún Umán's facilities and equipment. As we have mentioned, the Santa Ana Berlin base is still not complete. In addition, there have been persistent problems with the facilities that do exist there. For example, in early 2014, a transformer broke, and the base went for 15 days without electricity. The base authorities put in a request to MOD for a new transformer, but MOD never received it. They have also had problems with their water supply. Base personnel didn't have water for four months, during which they had to get their water from the firefighters in the community. Although the full explanation for problems with facilities requires further investigation, they are at least in part caused by the resourcing confusion and problems that persist between the MOG and MOD. Personnel at Santa Ana Berlin take these persistent problems to mean that the unit is not a priority for the Guatemalan government.

IATF Effectiveness

At the end of the IATF Tecún Umán 15-week initial training program in June 2013, the U.S. SCO and USARSOUTH representatives conducted an assessment of IATF capabilities based on a culminating capstone exercise. Five of the six METs (listed previously under "Training") were assessed. Of the five, Check Point Operations was the only task for which the IATF was assessed as "partially trained"; the IATF was assessed as "untrained" at Command and Control, Zone Reconnaissance, Cordon and Search, and Quick Reaction Force (Area Security was not assessed). Although the capstone exercise assessment offered feedback and discussion regarding the IATF's capabilities and shortfalls in each MET, it did not define full mission capability (FMC) or initial operating capability (IOC), nor did it explain the distinctions among "trained," "partially trained," and "untrained." It did, however, conclude that the IATF "demonstrated the basic skills to conduct tactical operations at the platoon level" but was not FMC according to U.S. standards.[2] No similar assessment has been conducted since then. The IATF Tecún Umán leadership agrees that although the United States has provided crucial initial training and assistance to set up the IATF, the Guatemalans should develop their own measures of effectiveness and assess the unit based on those measures. At the operational and tactical levels, IATF Tecún Umán military leaders explained that they have been conducting after-action reviews (AARs) following each operation or training cycle.

According to many in June 2014, IATF Tecún Umán was not being used for the missions it was designed to execute. Interviewees expressed their understanding of IATF Tecún Umán's mission as securing the border areas from trafficking and providing security for the population in those areas. Although IATF Tecún Umán has been participating in operations, its role in the operations has been limited to conducting patrols, running checkpoints, and providing perimeter security for other units responsible for actually executing the operation, such as the SGAIA. This is contrary to what the MOG and MOD leadership advertised in December 2013 as the intent of IATF Tecún Umán, which was to serve as an autonomous interagency unit capable of planning and executing operations in the border areas. According to many of the soldiers and police attached to IATF Tecún Umán, this is also how they understood their role and function. Although the current role may be appropriate given the remaining operational and tactical issues stemming from the dual-command problem and capability gaps as outlined earlier, this author saw no plan to develop the capability to operate as an autonomous interagency unit. Thus, senior leadership's bragging about all the "successful" IATF operations seems contrived and disingenuous to members of the IATF who feel they are not being used to their full potential. Some interviewees expressed opinions that senior leadership in Guatemala City was using IATF Tecún Umán to

---

[2] "Inter Agency Task Force (IATF) Tecún Umán—Guatemala (GTM) CAPSTONE Exercise Assessment–G3, Current Operations, Counter Transnational Threats (CTT), Counter Transnational Organized Crime (CTOC)," 2013.

show off, and for political purposes, rather than as a legitimate operational unit.[3] Regardless of the intent of IATF leadership in Guatemala City, this viewpoint's currency among at least some of the IATF Tecún Umán personnel means that the mission is not being clearly articulated throughout the force, and it could be negatively affecting morale of the troops and police on the ground.

---

[3] One interviewee expressed his opinion that the unit was not getting any results. "For appearances sake, it looks like there is good cooperation from the outside and from the higher levels, but the unit has not actually been achieving any operational results."

CHAPTER FOUR

Lessons and Main Findings

The IATF as it currently exists is still a nascent and evolving entity, but the Guatemalans have begun to apply key lessons to TF Chortí's formation and the plan for additional task forces. Furthermore, these lessons, presented in this chapter, are applicable across a broader spectrum of interagency task forces.

Lesson 1: The Importance of Establishing a Legal Framework Early

Creating a legal framework and documentation with support from all involved government agencies was important for gaining cooperation from all the entities involved in establishing IATF Tecún Umán. According to both Guatemalan and American interviewees, two factors were critical in the initial foundation of the IATF. The first was establishing the IATF Working Groups, which included key personnel from Guatemalan organizations involved in the IATF (MOG, MOD, SAT, MP, and OJ), and the U.S. SCO, which would facilitate key training from the United States to get the IATF off the ground. The second factor was having presidential support for a single chain of command and authority. However, the required legal documents were not issued until after the unit had been established and personnel had started working. Various sources agreed that the legal documents should have been created first, before the unit was set up. Doing this would have resolved many of the growing pains and challenges in the interagency relationships that were seen early in IATF development, such as initial tensions between MOD and MOG chains of command. Since the legal framework for the IATF is now in place, it will be easy to apply it to new IATFs as they are formed. Specifically, the key documents are

- *Acuerdo 277-2013*: This government agreement, which created the IATF, draws on the Guatemalan Constitution, as well as several other laws such as Decree 40-2000, the Act on Support to Civil Security Forces, to establish the authority to create the IATF. This agreement specifically defines the MOG as the head agency of the IATF, outlines required coordination from SAT, MP, and other state institutions, and lays out the powers assigned to the IATF. Refer to Appendix A for a translation of this agreement.
- *Acuerdo 563-2013*: This agreement defines the organization and operation of IATF based on Acuerdo 277-2013. It specifies the roles and relationships of the IATF Coordinator and IATF Commander and details coordination requirements, vehicle and equipment allocations, and subordinate organizations (such as the Information and Registration Center; see Lesson 3 following).

The Guatemalans heeded the important lesson of developing the legal framework early for IATF Chortí, as the Acuerdo was signed in April 2014 and the training did not start until July 2014. They signed the Acuerdo Gubernativo before the unit was formed and plan to sign the Acuerdo Ministerial before it begins operations. In addition, the Guatemalans have convened IATF Chortí Working Groups, although it was noted that MOD is not sending the appropriate level of leadership to these groups, and they have not yet been actively participating in the planning for IATF Chortí.

Lesson 2: The Need for Clearly Defined Interagency Relationships

The need for clear definitions of relationships between organizations involved is related to the requirement for a legal framework but goes further. The relationships in question must be conceptualized, executed, and institutionalized throughout the force. Building and developing the relationship between the police and military is a complex process that takes time, as does establishing and executing a strong relationship with other entities with a smaller presence in the IATF (SAT, MP, OJ).

The relationships with SAT, MP, and OJ for IATF Tecún Umán remained largely stagnant from December 2013 to June 2014. As the only personnel authorized to open and search locked containers, SAT agents represent a key node in operations that can either expedite or hinder a safe and successful operation. The model requires SAT to be closely involved; however, the mechanisms for this involvement are still undeveloped. There are SAT agents in the IATF HQ in Santa Ana Berlin. As mentioned earlier, to bring SAT to the table, it was not required to be an official signatory to Acuerdo 277-2013 and thus is not in the IATF chain of command. As a coordinating entity involved in the IATF, SAT agreed to assign eight of its agents to IATF Tecún Umán (there are currently five). These agents are attached to the IATF and were supposed to participate in operations with the unit. However, for SAT agents to be involved in any operations outside of the Tecún Umán area, IATF leadership must coordinate with SAT ahead of time and get explicit orders from SAT leadership. The roles and integration of MP and OJ are also very important in successful IATF operations. The Guatemalans explained their intent to have MP and OJ representatives colocated in a separate internal facility at the Tecún Umán base, and to review cases as they come in. However, as of June 2014, construction on the base was still ongoing, so colocation had not yet been achieved. It was unclear where these entities were or when they would be colocated.

Although seemingly little progress had been made in the SAT, MP, and OJ relationships in IATF Tecún Umán during the first half of 2014, the Guatemalans have been working to improve and strengthen these relationships for IATF Chortí. They plan to have a legal advisor, who represents the MP and OJ personnel attached to the IATF and works with the operations and logistics advisors as well as the IATF Coordinator (refer to Figure 2.4 in Chapter Two for the proposed organizational chart depicting these relationships).

Lesson 3: The Value of Developing an Organic Intelligence Capability

The Guatemalans recognize the importance of developing a legitimate and organic intelligence capability for the IATF. According to Acuerdo 563-2013, an Information and Registration Center (IRC) will be responsible for collecting and analyzing information used in planning IATF operations. As outlined in the Acuerdo, the Center will answer to the IATF Coordinator and will be based in Guatemala City. Each Guatemalan agency involved in the IATF will have a seat in the Center and will be able to monitor all operations. U.S. law enforcement will also be involved, and having all entities colocated will streamline communications and coordination. The Information and Registration Center will be subordinate to the Joint Intelligence Center (which will provide intelligence directly to the 5th Vice Minister).

In December 2013, Guatemalan leadership explained its plan to have a satellite intelligence group located in Tecún Umán, which would feed intelligence to the IRC in Guatemala City. However, as of June 2014, neither the IRC nor the satellite intelligence capability in Tecún Umán had been constructed or developed. The Guatemalan IATF leadership recognizes the importance of the IRC in integrating tactical- and operational-level intelligence to conduct operational planning. However, the ability of the IATF personnel to actually collect intelligence and feed it into an operational planning cycle is limited. This is not due to a lack of capability at the IATF level, as soldiers and police are constantly gathering tactical intelligence. Rather, it is because there is nowhere to feed this intelligence, and no established mechanism, at either Tecún Umán or higher levels, to act on the intelligence gathered or use it to plan operations. U.S. Army trainers conducting the tactical intelligence course in June 2014 reported that the soldiers and police they were training understood the basics of tactical intelligence collection. Students in this course commented that the training was very valuable for skill development, but since they never collected their own intelligence to conduct operations, they were unsure how they were going to use it. Indeed, several military interviewees explained that most of the IATF personnel are capable of gathering their own tactical intelligence, but that they had no support or authority to plan or conduct autonomous operations, so this limits their ability to react to any intelligence threats discovered.

In December 2013, the research team identified the need to establish the Information and Registration Center and Tecún Umán satellite intelligence capability. Taking into account the troubled history of illicit involvement of military intelligence units, with the close monitoring of the United States and provision of training and education on the appropriate use and process of collecting intelligence, the Guatemalans could develop a legitimate intelligence function. Training was provided to develop basic tactical- and operational-level intelligence capabilities in IATF Tecún Umán that can be incorporated into the planning cycle. As of June 2014, the Joint Intelligence Center was functioning but had limited capability. As a result, IATF Tecún Umán operations rely heavily on intelligence from SGAIA and MOG, which is less than ideal because these organizations are hesitant to readily share intelligence. In addition, there had been very little progress in setting up the tactical intelligence capability embodied in the IRC and satellite facility at Tecún Umán, outside of the intelligence training the U.S. Army provided in June. However, the Guatemalans have applied this lesson to plans to create an organic intelligence facility attached to the Command HQ (see Figure 4.1) of IATF Chortí that collects intelligence for the unit's operations.

Lesson 4: Transition to Police Authority and Leadership

Although IATF Tecún Umán leadership at the operational level (IATF Commander and below) consists of military personnel, police are being trained, educated, and primed to eventually take over the leadership roles. In the meantime, the stopgap solution of having a predominantly military leadership creates problems. Because of Guatemala's history of military rule and dominance, Guatemalan military and civilian entities alike are wary of the authority assigned to the military. For their part, the military personnel in IATF Tecún Umán expressed

Figure 4.1
IATF Chortí Command HQ Organization (Proposed)

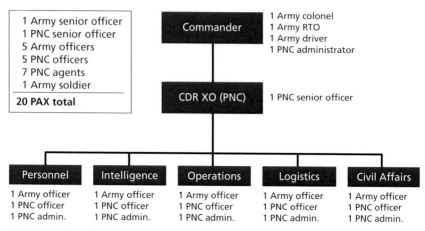

SOURCE: Adapted from U.S. SCO–Guatemala, 2014.
RAND RR885-4.1

their reluctance to give orders to police and to be perceived as trying to militarize the police/civilian security forces.

In December 2013, there was friction between the more seasoned police selected for the IATF Tecún Umán and the young military officers in charge of the companies and platoons. Since December, the Guatemalans have worked to replace some of the older police with younger police from the academy, intending to eventually bridge the leadership divide between the military and police chains. There were mixed perspectives on the effectiveness of this action in overcoming the friction. Some expressed the view that the new police are more capable, and there is better communication with them. However, others commented that they had seen no change, and still others explained that the new, younger police were actually less willing to work with the military and more biased against them. Still others explained that the relationship had started to improve but degenerated because of new police leadership who started segregating the military and police and not complying with military orders. These varying perspectives suggest that simply replacing a few of the police is not sufficient to overcome the friction.

Although in June 2014 there were supposedly two police officers (with the rank of lieutenant) assigned in leadership positions to IATF Tecún Umán, they do not operate as advisors or leaders at the military level, and rather function as a conduit to enforce orders from the military commanders down to the police. There is one police leader, a sub-inspector, located at Santa Ana Berlin, who is responsible for carrying out orders and all administrative affairs required of the police personnel assigned to IATF Tecún Umán. Frustrations were expressed by both military and police interviewees over disconnects in the chains of command and protocols for operations. Police explained that nowhere in the Acuerdo does it state that the police are subordinate to the military. Although the military leadership was intended as an interim solution, it is not apparent at the operational and tactical levels that there is a plan to transition to police leadership for IATF Tecún Umán. Current police leadership at IATF Tecún Umán expressed the need to have more police senior leaders (equivalent rank of the IATF Commander) attached to the unit to make decisions.

The Guatemalans have been working to produce capable police leaders. First, they are increasing police development capacity. The government has set up three additional police academies (up from one) and shortened the required basic training from one year to six months. This is part of President Molina's plan to grow the police force from 15,000 to 25,000 in four years. Second, 200 out of the 1,600 police who graduated in March 2014 were carefully selected to go to IATF Chortí. Finally, MOG and MOD hold ongoing discussions about making the executive officer (XO) a police billet in IATF Chortí (refer to Figure 4.1), but MOD has not signed off on the plan because of the issues it could generate with the chain of command. Although these are important initial steps for IATF Chortí's success, there does not seem to be a plan to resolve the tensions and discrepancies between the military and police at IATF Tecún Umán.

Lesson 5: The Need to Identify Measures of Effectiveness

In December 2013, the research team identified the need for the Guatemalans to develop measures of effectiveness (MOEs) for IATF Tecún Umán. Although it is important to track measures of performance (MOPs), such as number of operations, number of people arrested, and amounts of illegal drugs confiscated, it is crucial to develop MOEs to assess the impact and effectiveness of the IATF. These could include measures such as capability to integrate intelligence gathered at the tactical level into operational planning; ability to maintain various types of equipment; and ability for the IATF to conduct its own training. Another inherent part of measuring success is defining operational participation. In other words, how are the Guatemalans accounting for missions the IATF conducts? They currently consider a mission to be every time they go out, regardless of effect or impact. In that sense, they have conducted hundreds of missions. However, the U.S. SCO counts participation in far fewer missions—five in December 2013.

In June 2014, a unit in the MOG was tracking the operations and effects that the IATF had taken part in, but since the IATF has not led any of its own operations, its involvement could have been tangential or partial. Although this MOG unit has been measuring the effects of operations in which IATF Tecún Umán has been involved, that capability is not focused on the activities of the 5th Vice Minister's office, and there was no apparent coherent assessment process or MOE development for IATF Tecún Umán. The limited evaluation capability of the 5th Vice Minister's office is directed to assessing effects of operations and is currently tracking metrics such as number of crimes and level of security in various areas where IATF Tecún Umán has been involved. According to these metrics, IATF Tecún Umán has conducted ten operations so far this year. Despite the limited apparent assessment capability, however, the 5th Vice Minister's office and IATF leadership had made demonstrable progress in collecting data and measures focused specifically on the effects of the operations in which the IATF had participated in the first six months of 2014. In December 2013, these measures were focused on MOPs such as arrests and drugs confiscated, but in June 2014, these measures had expanded to MOEs such as decrease in crime rate and increase in security.[1] In addition, IATF leadership understood the importance of measuring the unit's success and explained requirements to regularly present evidence of IATF Tecún Umán's operational successes to Congress to maintain support and resources.

Lesson 6: The Importance of a Public Information Campaign

According to the Guatemalans, although successful operations and government investment are crucial for IATF sustainment, demonstrating this success and the value of the IATF to the Guatemalan people, especially those in the Tecún Umán area, is equally important. As mentioned previously, the population in border areas such as Tecún Umán is prospering and has been somewhat insulated from increasing violence of those complicit in the trafficking activities. In addition, local civilian authorities in Tecún Umán are alleged to be corrupt and coordinating with the DTOs in the area. Thus, residents along the border areas where IATF Tecún Umán intends to conduct operations need to be convinced of the value the IATF will provide for their security. The influence of the DTOs can be countered only through the genuine engagement of the IATF with the population to establish a positive state presence. This is an especially difficult challenge considering that the IATF will be operating in hostile territory where its targets essentially own the terrain, can exact revenge on the IATF members and their families, or offer them bribes to stay quiet.

Media coverage has been substantial, and the highest levels of government have shown public involvement.[2] The IATF Tecún Umán

---

[1]   This is based on discussions with the IATF Coordinator, who is also overseeing assessment efforts for IATF operations.

[2]   See, for example, "Guatemala Creará Fuerza Militar con Apoyo de EEUU para Combatir Narcotráfico," Univision, March 31, 2012; "Fuerza de Tarea Contrarrestará Contrabando en Frontera con México," Emisoras Unidas, December 16, 2013; and Brenda Larios, "Fuerza

launch ceremony on December 16, 2013, was attended by the highest-level government leadership and covered by several Guatemalan media agencies. However, it was unclear what the local population in Tecún Umán knew and understood about the IATF. The IATF's primary area of operations is actually the Tecún Umán population, and its support of IATF operations is, thus, crucial. Currently, IATF Tecún Umán does not have a designated Guatemalan public information campaign effort, so IATF leadership has been working with the U.S. Military Information Support Team (MIST) in Guatemala City to communicate the benefits of the IATF to the population with billboards, posters, and handbills. Along with a demonstrated ability to conduct operations, a comprehensive public information plan is needed. It is worth looking into developing the capability to formulate and implement such a plan within the Guatemalan IATF chain of command, which will be responsible for local outreach and for gaining the support of the Guatemalan population.

Lesson 7: The Importance of Equipment Maintenance

The Guatemalans have applied three very important equipment lessons from IATF Tecún Umán to IATF Chortí's development. First, because of problems that IATF Tecún Umán has had with the armored vehicles, IATF Chortí will have 46 nonarmored trucks. Second, the MOG is looking for ways to purchase 5.56mm machine guns, which the police can operate. This will allow for police attached to the IATF to fill more positions and is an important step in resolving some of the personnel and leadership discrepancies between the military and police. Third, an important lesson coming out of IATF Tecún Umán was the lack of assigned logistical support. Thus, IATF Chortí is planned to have a Service Support Company with mechanics devoted solely to IATF (refer to Figure 2.4 in Chapter Two). Finally, the MOG has signed for ownership of all the IATF Chortí vehicles, and the U.S. SCO is work-

---

de Tarea Tecún Umán Desarticula Nueve Bandas Criminales," Agencia Guatemalteca de Noticias, January 13, 2014.

ing with both the MOD and MOG to develop an agreement for the MOD to hand off all IATF Tecún Umán vehicles to the MOG.

CHAPTER FIVE

Challenges and Recommendations

As discussed in the previous section, the Guatemalan government has improved interagency relationships through development and progress on IATFs Tecún Umán and Chortí. However, several remaining challenges need to be addressed to achieve operational effectiveness and political sustainability. This section discusses those challenges and presents recommendations, for both the Guatemalans and the United States. Although we recognize the importance of Guatemalan autonomy and independence in making progress in IATF development, the United States has provided significant assistance to set up the IATFs and has a vested interest in ensuring the units' success, as well as accountability and ownership on the part of the Guatemalan government. Thus, the recommendations here can serve as possible milestones of progress that can be used to evaluate the benefit of continued U.S. involvement.

Challenge 1: Resolve the Duality-of-Command Issue

Although the Acuerdo was a substantial accomplishment in bringing agencies together, if it is not understood, disseminated, and institutionalized, it has very little value beyond symbolic. An agreement on its own is not sufficient to get full cooperation from agencies, especially to bridge the long-standing divide between the MOD and MOG. In June 2014, the MOD and MOG still could not agree on a way to align duties and authority when it came to IATF Tecún Umán, and these effects were proliferating throughout the unit. Many agreed that legal guidance is not understood nor followed by all parties. An effective relationship between the military and police at all levels requires a clear definition and delineation of the chain of command.

Recommendations for Guatemala

Guatemalan leadership needs to ensure each level understands and supports associated roles and responsibilities, from the most senior leader to the most junior soldier and police agent on the ground. Three major events or steps should be considered:

1. Conduct a meeting at the highest levels of leadership (MOG/5th Vice Minister, MOD/CHOD) that results in all parties agreeing on the operational chain of command and to execute and disseminate it among their personnel. Ideally, an official document, or Convenio, will be developed that clearly defines the roles and relationships of each IATF Tecún Umán level and rank.
2. Ask senior leaders from the MOG and MOD chains to brief the entire IATF (both military and police) on the chain of command, as well as consequences for not following that chain of command.
3. Identify toxic leaders (on both the military and police sides), and either indoctrinate them into the new agreed-upon chain of command, roles, and responsibilities, or remove them from their leadership positions.

Recommendations for the United States

The U.S. SCO in Guatemala has been actively involved in IATF Tecún Umán and IATF Chortí. Representatives from the SCO have participated in the working groups for both IATFs and have worked closely with representatives from both the MOG and MOD to define and agree upon interagency relationships. A meeting occurred in July 2014 between the 5th Vice Minister, CHOD, and the U.S. SCO Deputy Chief, which was a preliminary step to resolve the MOG-MOD duality-of-command issue. U.S. involvement should continue in order to ensure accountability for resolving the MOG-MOD relationship problems. This includes ensuring the official document defining the chain of command is signed and accepted by all parties, and that it is briefed and understood at all levels of the IATF. The SCO can influence this process both through its close relationships at the strategic level (MOD and MOG/5th Vice Ministry), as well as the continual tactical training it provides to IATF personnel.

Challenge 2: Improve Operational Planning Capability

According to key representatives in the U.S. SCO, one of the major gaps inhibiting the ability for IATF Tecún Umán to conduct timely and relevant missions is the lack of operational planning capability at the 5th Vice Minister level and below. There is no operational cell at the 5th Vice Minister level and an insufficient number of personnel with the military planning and operational expertise to be able to coordinate operations and lead the planning for the IATF. Because of the lack of operational planning capability at the ministerial level, the IATF has been functioning as a reactionary unit, rather than being able to get out front and execute operations. However, this extends to below the ministerial level as well. As the unit on the front lines, the IATF should be feeding information into and providing feedback on the operational planning cycle. Several individuals interviewed at the operational and tactical levels explained that even if they were able to collect actionable intelligence and develop a plan at the task force level, they would not be able to plan or conduct an operation, since all planning occurs at the level of the 5th Vice Minister's office.

Since the IATF is not recognized as an intelligence gathering entity, the intelligence collected on the ground is not incorporated into operational planning. Part of this problem is also that the 5th Vice Minister's office does not have its own intelligence capabilities but rather gets information from MOG, which is difficult because there is sensitivity about sharing intelligence within the MOG. Thus, the 5th Vice Minister's office has to use MOD channels at times, which leads to imperfect and sometimes outdated intelligence. This lack of organic intelligence capability is a major issue that needs to be resolved if the IATF is to develop into a functional and effective unit. Although the Guatemalans had concrete plans to develop the IRC in December 2013, the SCO withdrew its support because of concerns over its using the intelligence capabilities for illegitimate purposes. Given the decades of history and continued problems with an abuse of intelligence functions and capabilities for financial and political gain, as discussed previously, these concerns are well founded. As one of the contributing factors to the failures of previous similar units, this problem is not easy to fix. It would require an entirely new approach and structure to the Guatemalan intelligence apparatus. However, recognizing the importance of sound and reliable intelligence, if the decision is made to continue to invest in developing a legitimate Guatemalan intelligence capability, close involvement and monitoring by the United States would be required.

Recommendations for Guatemala

The Guatemalans should work with the U.S. SCO to set up an operational planning cell in the 5th Vice Ministry and identify and vet operational planners with the military expertise necessary to plan IATF operations. This operational planning cell should set up an operational planning cycle that incorporates intelligence and planning capability from the tactical and operational levels at Tecún Umán. In addition, the Guatemalans should continue with plans to set up the IRC, as well as the tactical intelligence facility at Tecún Umán.

Recommendations for the United States

USSOUTHCOM and USARSOUTH should work with the SCO to embed U.S. military planning experts in the 5th Vice Minister's office as part of the operations cell to advise on the process. One of the options for this is the Ministry of Defense Advisors (MoDA) program.[1]

---

[1]   This program partners the U.S. Department of Defense civilian experts with foreign counterparts to build ministerial core competencies such as personnel and readiness, logistics, strategy and policy, and financial management. For more information, refer to the Defense Security Cooperation Agency's Ministry of Defense Advisors home page online.

In addition, the SCO should work with the Guatemalans to develop an operational cell in the 5th Vice Minister's office that is responsible for coordinating across departments in planning operations for the IATF and ensure that cell is staffed with experienced military planners able to operate at the ministerial level. Finally, the SCO and other involved U.S. parties should determine acceptable involvement in setting up the IRC and continue to work with the Guatemalans to secure with personnel in Tecún Umán a legitimate intelligence feedback loop that will inform operational planning. If the decision is made to assist in development of IATF intelligence capabilities, the U.S. SCO and other entities should clearly define under what conditions, with what controls, and under whose authority that development will happen, and what mechanisms can prevent abuse of any intelligence skills or capabilities.

Challenge 3: Develop an Organic Training Capability

IATF Tecún Umán has received exceptional training from a variety of U.S. organizations and in a wide range of areas. However, the Guatemalans recognize the importance of the capacity to train, develop, and sustain their own force. In order to do this, both the United States and the Guatemalans have identified the need to train Guatemalan instructors to conduct their own training for incoming IATF personnel. In June 2014, this concept was still in its infancy, and the plan to implement a train-the-trainer program had not yet been developed. Setting up this program and organic training capability will be important as the Guatemalans turn their attention to establishing IATF Chortí and additional IATFs. Key representatives from the U.S. SCO expressed the desire to stand up a Guatemalan Mobile Training Team (MTT) capable of providing level 1 (basic) skill training, so that the IATFs can sustain themselves at the basic level. The United States would then focus on providing specialized and advanced skill training.

Recommendations for Guatemala
The Guatemalans should identify capable and qualified instructors to take over basic training, beginning with the Guatemalan trainers

already involved in initial IATF training. In addition, they should work with the U.S. SCO and other U.S. trainers to develop and execute a train-the-trainer plan for basic skill training.

Recommendations for the United States

U.S. involvement and assistance to develop a Guatemalan basic training capability is crucial in ensuring the sustainability of the IATF. USSOUTHCOM and USARSOUTH should work with the SCO to develop and execute train-the-trainer courses to develop organic training capability so Guatemalans can train their own forces, which should be accompanied by a plan and timeline to transition this basic training capability to the Guatemalans. Concurrently, the U.S. SCO should continue to provide training through the JPAT and other specialized training courses.

Challenge 4: Address Corruption Problems

Corruption remains a major issue within the Guatemalan government. As discussed earlier, corruption throughout the police and military ranks has allowed DTOs to continue to operate along the border areas and throughout the country with impunity. If not properly addressed and remedied, these corruption problems could stymie any continued progress of the IATF concept and could lead to its failure.

The U.N.-led International Commission Against Impunity in Guatemala (CICIG), created in 2007, supports Guatemala's prosecution of individuals involved in criminal organizations operating within state institutions and builds the capacity of the Guatemalan justice sector institutions.[2] In addition, the United States is working with the Guatemalan Police Reform Commission to address police reform and professionalize the National Civil Police.[3] Working through the Central American Regional Security Initiative (CARSI), the U.S. has been helping the Guatemalans expand their capabilities to interdict, inves-

---

[2] For more information, see the CICIG website.

[3] DoS, 2013.

tigate, and prosecute illicit trafficking.[4] There have been ample problems with police corruption in the past, but efforts are being made to address them. For example, the CICIG has helped counter some of the rampant corruption, launching investigations that have resulted in the dismissal of 2,000 members of the National Civilian Police and the arrest and prosecution of a number of senior government and state officials.[5] Additionally, in 2013 the 5th Vice Minister launched an investigation against 14 antinarcotics police on corruption charges. The 5th Vice Minister oversaw the investigation, and all 14 suspects were tried, found guilty of corruption charges, and put in prison. There is currently a strict vetting procedure for personnel entering the IATF, including psychological, medical, and polygraph examinations. The 5th Vice Minister does the vetting, with the assistance of the U.S. SCO. However, to guarantee the legitimacy of the IATF, the police corruption must continue to be mitigated and controlled so that it is not a potential source of conflict in IATF operations.

Recommendations for Guatemala

The 5th Vice Ministry should continue to crack down on corruption in the police force while implementing the stringent vetting procedures for police personnel entering the IATF. In addition, the MOG should ensure that the influx of police officers being trained and produced at the police academies is indoctrinated on the dangers of corruption and how to avoid it.

Recommendations for the United States

The United States should continue to work with the Guatemalans on maintaining stringent vetting procedures, investigating corruption charges, and ensuring that the new police academies being set up around the country are closely complying with the new regulations to prevent corruption.

---

[4] DoS, 2014.

[5] International Crisis Group Latin America, 2010.

Challenge 5: Address IATF Tecún Umán Issues Before Refocusing Efforts to IATF Chortí

The unanimous opinion among Guatemalans and Americans alike in June 2014 was that the Guatemalans are rushing the creation of IATF Chortí. President Molina wants IATF Chortí to be operational before the end of 2014 to demonstrate its value in advance of the 2016 elections; however, the buildings and equipment will not be complete until mid-2015, so IATF Chortí will be operating under capacity and not reach full operational capability until mid-2015. Although some crucial lessons from IATF Tecún Umán have been applied in IATF Chortí's development, the reason for creating IATFs sequentially was to develop a model and then refine it. However, that does not seem to be the actual approach. It seems as if the Guatemalans have shifted focus from IATF Tecún Umán to IATF Chortí.

Recommendations for Guatemala

The Guatemalans should focus efforts on resolving the major problems that prevent IATF Tecún Umán from conducting autonomous operations. Although IATF Chortí is the priority from the Guatemalan perspective, the efforts of IATF Tecún Umán should not be wasted.

Recommendations for the United States

The United States has contributed a substantial amount of financial assistance ($22.5 million in total, including about $15 million from USSOUTHCOM) to the development of IATF Tecún Umán. Therefore, the United States has a vested interest in ensuring the unit's success. Although the Guatemalans have planned for the financial sustainment of IATF Chortí in their budget, USSOUTHCOM is still contributing $13.4 million to assist in initial development. Continued funding should be contingent on resolving issues that limit the effectiveness of IATF Tecún Umán.

CHAPTER SIX

Conclusion

The Guatemalans have made important strides since IATF Tecún Umán was conceptualized. Although there are challenges and outstanding issues between the MOG and MOD, the formation of the IATF has helped strengthen interagency cooperation. The Acuerdo is the first time the organizations have come together to sign a legally binding document. In conjunction with the Acuerdo, several other factors have given IATF Tecún Umán a better chance of success than its predecessors, including better vetting and training (with the assistance of the United States) and more political will from top leadership. To sustain this momentum, it is worth continued U.S. investment in developing IATF capabilities, including assisting the successful establishment of IATF Chortí.

The United States has contributed substantial sums to implementing the IATF concept, and the Guatemalans have committed the funding to sustain Chortí and additional IATFs. The political will currently exists among key Guatemalan leadership to move the IATF process forward, as evidenced by President Molina's emphasis on countering corruption in his ministries, strengthening and legitimizing the police force, and developing a force that can effectively take on the DTOs. The IATF concept was envisioned, executed, and institutionalized by the Molina administration, which will be in office until 2016. Our sources agree that if the IATF can continue with its current momentum, it will demonstrate its value and be sustained through future administrations. Thus, President Molina has been pushing IATF Chortí to be up and running before the election cycle begins (the next elections are scheduled in September 2015). If both IATF Tecún Umán and Chortí are operational and effective by the end of his term, there is a good chance there will be enough momentum to sustain them through the next presidency. However, the operational success of IATF Tecún Umán at this juncture is questionable, and although there is political will at the highest levels of the government for its sustainability, this is not mirrored at key positions further down the chain of command.

The United States should be thinking about the long term and pressing Guatemala to leverage the political will that exists in the Molina administration to develop the institutional capacity and legitimate relationships and practices for the Guatemalans to sustain the IATFs on their own. But for the IATF to become sustainable, the Guatemalans require continued U.S. involvement, at least in the near term, to ensure commitment through the next administration, and the United States must do its part. Given the history of U.S. relations with Guatemala, which have not always been consistent, the Guatemalans are concerned that here, too, the U.S. commitment will not be sustained long enough to bear fruit. However, as long as Guatemala remains one of USSOUTHCOM's top priorities, it seems likely that the United States' support will not lag and that it will, therefore, be sufficient to follow through with the entire IATF concept. Beyond that, it is truly up to the Guatemalans.

Translation of Acuerdo 277-2013

Acuerdo 277-2013[1]

MINISTRY OF INTERIOR

Agreed to create the Interagency Task Force of Tecún Umán

GOVERNMENT AGREEMENT NUMBER 277-2013

Guatemala, July 25, 2013

THE PRESIDENT OF THE REPUBLIC
CONSIDERING

That the Political Constitution of the Republic of Guatemala establishes, among others, as fundamental duties of the state as the life, safety and peace, organizing to protect the person and the family, and its supreme goal the realization of the common good.

CONSIDERING

Decree Number 40-2000 of the Congress of the Republic, Act on the Support to Civil Security Forces, provides that the Civil Security Forces will be supported in their duties to prevent and combat orga-

---

[1] Translated by RAND research assistant.

nized crime for the Military Units of Guatemala deemed necessary when circumstances demand the country's security assistance.

CONSIDERING

It is the duty of the State to increase and strengthen the measures to prevent, disrupt, eradicate, and effectively combat various forms of organized crime and common crime; making necessary the creation of an organization that develops implementing combined operations throughout the Republic of Guatemala, so the issue of government regulation creating the corresponding interagency task force is necessary.

THEREFORE

In the exercise of the functions that are conferred on it by Articles 183 a) and e) of the Political Constitution of the Republic of Guatemala; and on the basis of Articles 27 j) and k), 36 m) and n) and 37 d) of Decree No. 114-97 of the Congress of the Republic of Guatemala, Law of the Executive Agency; 1 and 2 of Decree No. 40-2000 of the Congress of the Republic of Guatemala, Act on the Support to Civil Security Forces.

AGREES

Article 1. Creation. This creates the Interagency Task Force Tecún Umán.

Article 2. Object. The Intergovernmental Task Force Tecún Umán is intended to conduct combined security operations throughout the Republic in order to prevent, combat, dismantle, and eradiate criminal actions.

Article 3. Integration. The Intergovernmental Task Force Tecún Umán also integrates:

　　A) Ministry of Governance

　　B) Ministry of National Defense.

Article 4. Interagency Cooperation. The Intergovernmental Task Force Tecún Umán, for the achievement of its objectives, may coordinate with the Public Ministry, Superintendencia de Administración Tributaria (SAT), and other state institutions as well as with national and international entities deemed relevant.

Article 5. Coordination. The Coordination of the Interagency Task Force Tecún Umán will be the charge of the Ministry of Interior, through the Minister, who may delegate it to one of the deputy ministers in the branch.

Article 6. Powers. The following are the duties of the Interagency Task Force Tecún Umán:

> a) Strengthen the prevention of crimes in the country with priority in border areas, and in areas of a high incidence of common or organized crime;
>
> b) Perform operations that allow the dismantlement, eradication, and combating of criminal actions with priority given to areas along the borders and in areas with a high incidence of common or organized crime;
>
> c) Generate protocols in order to define performance criteria in the different procedures, taking into consideration the effect already established by each of the participating Ministries in compliance with the legislation in force;
>
> d) Define interagency channels of coordination; and
>
> e) Any other functions as may be necessary to establish compliance with the benefit of its creation.

Article 7. Resources. The institutions that are part of the Interagency Task Force Tecún Umán or coordinate some of their activities with it, can manage the resources required for their participation in this Task Force within its draft budget expenditures; thus, the Interagency Cooperation Agreements can be observed in the finance of those same activities.

Article 8. Internal Provisions. Within 60 days after the date of the term of this agreement, the Coordination of the Interagency Task Force Tecún Umán must issue the ministerial agreement containing the Rules for its organization and functioning.

Article 9. Effectiveness. The Government Decision shall take effect the day following its publication in the Journal of Central America.

Bibliography

Center for Naval Analysis, "Criminal Organizations and Illicit Trafficking in Guatemala's Border Communities," IPR 15225, December 2011.

CICIG [International Commission Against Impunity in Guatemala], website, undated, as of November 17, 2014:
http://www.cicig.org/index.php?page=home

———, *Sixth Report of Activities of the International Commission Against Impunity in Guatemala (CICIG)*, September 2012–August 2013.

Fraser, General Douglas M., United States Air Force, Commander, US Southern Command, posture statement before the 112th Congress, House Armed Services Committee, March 6, 2012.

"Fuerza de Tarea Contrarrestará Contrabando en Frontera con México," Emisoras Unidas, December 16, 2013. As of November 14, 2014:
http://noticias.emisorasunidas.com/noticias/nacionales/
fuerza-tarea-contrarrestara-contrabando-frontera-mexico

Griffin, Jennifer, "America's Third War: Fighting Drug Cartels in Guatemala," Fox News, December 13, 2010. As of November 13, 2014:
http://www.foxnews.com/us/2010/12/13/
americas-war-fighting-drug-cartels-guatemala/

"Guatemala Creará Fuerza Militar con Apoyo de EEUU para Combatir Narcotráfico," Univision, March 31, 2012. As of November 14, 2014:
http://feeds.univision.com/feeds/article/2012-03-31/
guatemala-creara-fuerza-militar-con?refPath=/noticias

Guatemalan Ministry of Governance, "Presentación Fuerza Tarea Tecún Umán," briefing, July 8, 2013.

"Inter Agency Task Force (IATF) Tecún Umán—Guatemala (GTM) CAPSTONE Exercise Assessment–G3, Current Operations, Counter Transnational Threats (CTT), Counter Transnational Organized Crime (CTOC)," conducted by U.S. Army South G3 CUOPS–Counter Transnational Organized Crime (CTOC), July 2013.

International Crisis Group, *Guatemala: Squeezed Between Crime and Impunity*, Latin America Report No. 33, June 22, 2010.

————, *Guatemala: Drug Trafficking and Violence*, Latin America Report No. 39, October 11, 2011.

Larios, Brenda, "Fuerza de Tarea Tecún Umán Desarticula Nueve Bandas Criminales," Agencia Guatemalteca de Noticias, January 13, 2014. As of November 14, 2014:
http://www.agn.com.gt/index.php/reportajes-especiales/item/11939-fuerza-de-tarea-tecún-umán-desarticula-nueve-bandas-criminales

López, Julie, "Guatemala's Crossroads: Democratization of Violence and Second Chances," Working Paper Series on Organized Crime in Central America, Woodrow Wilson Center for International Scholars, December 2010.

"Rethinking the Drug War in Central America and Mexico: Analysis and Recommendations for Legislators," The Mesoamerican Working Group (MAWG), November 2013.

U.S. Department of Defense, Defense Security Cooperation Agency, Ministry of Defense Advisors, web page, undated. As of November 17, 2014:
http://www.dsca.mil/programs/ministry-defense-advisors

U.S. Department of State, Bureau of International Narcotics and Law Enforcement Affairs, *Guatemala*, 2013 International Narcotics Control Strategy Report, March 5, 2013. As of November 13, 2014:
http://www.state.gov/j/inl/rls/nrcrpt/2013/vol1/204049.htm

————, Bureau of International Narcotics and Law Enforcement Affairs, *Country Report: Guatemala*, 2014 International Narcotics Control Strategy Report, 2014. As of November 13, 2014:
http://www.state.gov/j/inl/rls/nrcrpt/2014/vol1/222894.htm

U.S. Government Accountability Office, *U.S. Agencies Considered Various Factors in Funding Security Activities, but Need to Assess Progress in Achieving Interagency Objectives*, Washington, D.C., GAO-13-771, September 2013.

U.S. Security Cooperation Office–Guatemala, "Interagency Border Unit," brief, April 3, 2013.

————, "IATF-Chortí," brief, June 9, 2014.